ASHLEY

Crochet
FOR BEGINNERS

book description

Do you want to make a beautiful, lacy crochet piece? Or do you want to create comfy, chunky blankets and shawls but afraid that you won't be able to learn how to crochet? Stop worrying and get comfortable because *Crochet for Beginners* is here to make learning crochet easy and fun!

In crochet for beginners, you'll find out

- How crochet is done, and why it's so much easier than it looks

- How to crochet as a beginner whether you're left- or right-handed

- How to make beginner-friendly yet expert-looking blankets, throws, pillows, shawls, toys, and decorations

- How to choose best tools and supplies

- How to plan and organize your crochet craft

- And so much more!

This book teaches you to read crochet patterns so that you can make any pattern you find online—whether free or paid. Even better, this book provides illustrations and instructions so that you know exactly how your work should look! No confusion, no frustration—only joy!

Order *Crochet for Beginners* right now, and start making dozens of beginner patterns and stitches that are waiting inside!

crochet for beginners

Discover How To Easily Crochet From Scratch. Learn And Use The Best Techniques To Create Incredible Projects, Even If You Don't Have Any Crocheting Experience

- Ashley Cotton -

3

table of contents

introduction

Do you want to learn how to crochet? Do you want something fun and productive to do at the end of the workday? If so, this is the crochet manual for you! In this book, you'll find out how to crochet even if you've never held a needle. You'll learn what tools and supplies to get, how to read crochet diagrams, patterns, and instructions, and so much more! You'll get the basics of popular stitches down so that you can tackle any project you desire.

This book gives you detailed explanations for how crochet is done from choosing yarn and hooks to finding the right size for your work. If you're a fan of weaving, knitting, and embroidery, then crochet is the best hobby for you! It's fun and easy but has a lot of history and meaning. Thanks to archeological finds, scientists traced crochet back to tombs of Old Norse people! As it turned out, crochet hooks were around for much longer than it's commonly known.

However, crochet wasn't the same craft that it was in its early days. It is said that modern crochet as we know it began developing during the 16th century. At first it was used in France to make lace. However, samples of true crochet were found among Guiana Indians, which indicated that the craft existed for much longer than we're familiar with. There are different theories about how crochet came to be; however, many of them agree that the craft originated in Southeast Asia. Traces of crochet were found not only in the Mediterranean but also in South America, East Asia, and even China!

Most researchers agree that China can be considered to be the first original home to crochet. From there, the craft was adopted across Turkey, Persia, North Africa, and India. Once the crochet arrived in Europe, it was first done on a backup fabric and called tambour. Somewhere around the 18th century, people stopped using the background fabric and began working the stitches on their own. This was when the term 'crochet' was coined, and it had numerous advantages over 'tambour.' It didn't require as much time, and it was also done on much bigger needles, which made the work simpler and more comfortable.

Crochet spread from Europe during the early 1800s and eventually arrived in the UK and the US. Pattern books were popular and sold widely, as many women wanted the opportunity for not only a fun hobby but also to decorate clothing and their homes with useful, good-quality designs.

Crochet only requires two basic tools: a hook and yarn, but you can also include add ons for a more complex design. You can crochet successfully on any budget and regardless of how much time you have at your disposal. You can crochet all sorts of yarn from thin and silky to soft and chunky. Luckily for you, you no longer have to manage with hemp, linen, and metal threads. Today's yarn is much better quality and elegant and is either synthetic or cotton-based. Even better, you can also look for hypoallergenic yarn, which is safe for anyone with sensitivities as well as babies and small children.

There's much more variety in the needle selection as well. Nowadays, you can pick and choose between plastic, wooden, and metal needles that are safe and easy to use. In the past, people used fish and animal bones as well as horns and numerous metals to create crochet hooks. These yarns and needles were used to make practical handwork, clothing, throws, blankets, and bags, fishnets, and much more. During the 16th century and onwards, people began using crochet to make covers and throws, shawls, shades, lamp mats, and even rugs.

We have a richness of hooks and yarn at our disposal to make beautiful crochet items of your choosing. You can go for decoration, clothing, and even toys. In this book, you'll find instructions with illustrations to make cute sculptures and useful clothing items that are comparable to expert-level design and quality.

But before we can begin anything fancy, we need to start with the basics. We'll first go over how to read a pattern and some common stitches you will encounter. Once you know how to decode different stitches and steps needed to complete a piece, it's only a matter of time and preference as to which project you would like to choose. We'll discuss the tools and supplies necessary for different projects, which hooks work best with different types of yarn, and what yarn suits your needs best for each project. Regardless of whether you're left or right-handed, the instructions will be suited for both, so don't let this trouble you or keep you from taking the first step.

You picked up this book to learn a new craft, and that's exactly what we're going to talk about. What you probably weren't expecting was a stress-relieving, mind-calming practice that you can take practically anywhere. Crochet is proven to benefit both your physical and mental health. It will help you wind down after a hard day's work, release anxiety, and soothe down for a night of restful sleep. If you've been struggling to go to bed on time, doing crochet for an hour or two in the evening keeps your eyes away from the harmful blue light from electronic devices. Resting your eyes and letting the natural light from the setting sun trigger your brain for sleep is a much more beneficial evening activity than scrolling social media or watching videos. Crochet is also found to help people feel overall happier and more satisfied. If you were looking for the sort of entertainment to lift your spirits, this might be the right craft! Crochet also keeps your mind active, engaged, and stimulated. It helps train focus and intellectual abilities, which is why crochet is considered to be a beneficial prevention for dementia, memory problems, and overall helpful for mental stimulation.

So what are you waiting for? Grab your tools now and start reading!

chapter 1
How to Read Crochet Patterns

You might have come across easy-to-follow videos and written instructions, where you only model after the instructor and follow their steps. But what happens if you want to make a very specific piece, and there's no one to show you how to do it? If you want to learn how to crochet fully independently, you'll need to learn how to read the patterns first. Crochet patterns give you an idea how making an entire piece from scratch will look like, what stitches are needed and how many of them, what sort of hook and yarn to use, and whatever necessary information is needed to try to replicate the piece.

Reading Crochet Patterns: What's in Your Diagram?

A crochet pattern is a collection of written instructions, symbols, and abbreviations that display the series of stitches that you'll use to create a piece. Patterns often, if not always, feature crochet diagrams that give you a graphic representation of what the work will look like. Seemingly, this is an easy and straightforward way to crochet. Sadly, many beginners become intimidated by abbreviations and symbols, but it's not uncommon. In this chapter, you will learn how to read patterns and diagrams so that you're able to make any chosen piece regardless of the design or difficulty.

Crochet Symbols

Crochet symbols are drawings of stitches that indicate the sequences that will be done in a diagram. Symbols indicate different types of stitches that, combined with other abbreviations and other symbols, create the design that you're trying to make. It's of utmost importance to include each stitch into your design without skipping. Every stitch has a role to play in the design, and skipping stitches can cause your work to come out uneven or with visible flaws.

Difficulty levels

Crochet patterns can be roughly divided into beginner/easy, intermediate, and advanced categories. The beginner-friendly patterns are simple and easy to make. They either consist of one or two alternating stitches or sequences or stitches that are simple to learn. The greater the difficulty of the pattern, the greater the complexity of the work. If you're newer to the scene, begin with some beginners patterns and work your way up to more complex designs. Doing so will get you used to the feel of the needles when making certain stitches, will familiarize you with how to transition to new sequences, and help you understand symbols so that it comes naturally in more complex designs.

When working on more advanced pieces, don't feel discouraged if you have to look up the basics every now and then. Even advanced crocheters still make mistakes. Pace yourself, and remember that this is a hobby that is meant to relax. Take your time with complex pieces because it's better to go slow and steady than try to speed through a piece.

Necessary Tools

Aside from the crochet diagram, your pattern will include a list of materials and supplies needed for the work. It will contain information about the necessary yarn weight, length, and color as well as the hook type and size. Some patterns also tell you whether to use tapestry needles and stitch markers as well. However, the most important information found in the crochet pattern concerns the size, length, and weight of the yarn. With a variety of different yarns and brands available, following these instructions will ensure that you get the right yarn for the project and achieve the right results regardless of the brand.

Different types and sizes of yarn reflect on a desired choice of the hook as well. Your crochet pattern will also include the size and the type of hook that you should use. Patterns also show what add-ons you can use if you wish and what size of these add-ons works best with the design. This is important because most people want to create unique work and personalize the design so that it doesn't come out the same as millions of others. Add-ons allow you to slightly alter the appearance of the design and give it a more unique flare.

Crochet Gauge

It's not always easy to determine the desired size of your work. Different labels of the same size and weight yarn can be harder or softer compared to one another, and they can also stretch to different degrees. All of this makes it a lot more difficult to determine how many stitches you need for a particular crochet size. Some blanket designs, for example, consist of simple stitching sequences, and the pattern gives you a small-to-mid dimension as a sort of framework that you can later increase or decrease as needed.

But let's say that the size of your work also depends on the size of your bed, couch, or table. In that case, you need to adjust the pattern to the size of the work. This is done easily when you know the gauge. Gauging is a simple measurement that shows you how many stitches you need for a certain size, like one to five inches. To check the gauge, you need to crochet a pattern piece and compare it to the sample from the diagram. If your sample is too large, you need to reduce the size of the hook or increase it if your pattern is smaller than the one in the diagram.

Another piece of information that you'll find in the crochet diagrams concerns the sizing of the finished work. With some items, like clothing and covers, you need options regarding the size in case the pattern is too big or too small for you. That way, all you need to do is follow written instructions, and your item will fit you perfectly. Usually, crochet patterns indicate sizes either in brackets '()' or '/'. Once you've determined the size from the sample that you wish to make, you can then highlight it on the diagram using a marker to simplify the process and reduce errors while crocheting.

Stitches and Motifs

Crochet patterns contain stitch sets that you can review and plan before you start

13

working. For example, you can check how many different stitches a pattern has. Then you can exercise these different stitches to get ready for a seamless, relaxing crochet. Furthermore, different series and sets of stitches create motifs. When the work has one or several different motifs, it's useful to plan how to do them. For example, you can start from the easiest ones to slowly warm up until you reach the more complex parts of the design.

Reading Instructions: Learn the Stitching Language

The written instructions are the largest part of the pattern. They offer a written version of the movements, stitches, and sequences that the project calls for. Once you learn how to read instructions, they will be easy to follow, and you can make them even easier by dividing the work into rounds, parts, or sub-pieces. Do what works best for you! The instructions also reveal different stages of the work using abbreviations. Here's the list of the most common abbreviations used in crochet patterns with their meaning:

- Ss or "sl st"—slip stitch

- Ch—chain

- Dc/sc—single (UK) or double (US) crochet

- Tr/dc—treble crochet in UK terminology or double crochet for US terminology

- Htr/Htc—half-treble (UK) or half-double (US) crochet

- Dtr/tr—double treble (UK) or treble (US) crochet

- Ttr/Dtr—triple treble (UK) or double treble (US) crochet

- Gauge (US) or Tension (UK)

- Increase (inc) or decrease (dec)

- Front post (fp) and back post (bp)

- Front loop (fl) and back loop (bl)

- Skip (US) or miss/skip (UK)

- Fasten off—a phrase common to both US and UK crochet that means to tie up and cut off thread once you're done with the work or an individual piece.

The meanings of the abbreviations are straightforward, and once you get a hand of stitches and loops, you'll be able to read them easily. However, reading the instructions becomes a bit more difficult when they're laid out one next to the other, with added numbers that show how many of each stitch or action to make. To avoid getting caught in the middle of the work and not knowing what to crochet next, it's best that you first study a pattern and discover how many parts or sequences it consists of, and then just focus on a single part until you've finished it.

The 'row' simply means a row of crochet stitches in the work or a line from the beginning to the end of a row. The term 'round' means a circle. Technically, a round is the same type of stitching series needed for a row, but it's done in a circular shape. Unlike rows, you don't finish a round at the other end or edge of the work, but instead you get back to the first loop you made while you were beginning making that round. Then you crochet one or several stitches into that first/last loop and turn over the work to begin the next circular round.

At the beginning of your pattern, you will notice an instruction to make a slip stitch or a slip knot. This knot, which you'll learn how to make later in the book, is the first loop of your work that serves as a base for your first row or round. However, not all patterns contain this instruction. Some go on an assumption that you know that work begins with a slip knot, so make sure to make one first even if it's not in the instructions. Some patterns show which patterns repeat and how many times, although this isn't always the case.

Usually crochet patterns start with a number that indicates how many chain stitches you need for your foundation chain. A foundation chain is the base of your work and consists of plain slip stitches. The pattern will indicate "Foundation chain: XY," or "foundation chain multiples of X+Y." The first instruction means that you need to crochet an XY number of loops, and the second shows you how many loops you can repeat in a pattern. Upon reading this instruction, you need to make a required number of chain stitches or loops. With the base chain, you don't count the slip knot into stitches.

Once you're finished working on your foundation chain, the pattern then shows you what stitches to crochet for the first row. For example, if it says to do "2ch, sc, skip 1, rep," it means that, when you begin a row, you first need to "chain two," or make two chain stitches, and then weave the last loop of that stitch into the foundation chain with a single stitch. After that, you need to skip one loop, do another two-chain and weave it into the next loop, and proceed to do so until the end of the row. Once you finish the row, count the stitches again to see if your count matches the pattern, but don't count the loop that remains on your hook. I advise beginners to count stitches after each row to ensure that they haven't skipped any.

When you see the word 'turn' on your pattern, that means that the row is over and you should turn the work to start another one. When you're turning over the work, make sure that your hook is still in the work so that you don't lose your remaining loop. Depending on the pattern, the instruction for starting the next row may or may not be printed out. A common way to start a new row is to turn and chain one stitch and only then start with the stitching by instruction for that row. If that instruction isn't in the pattern, make sure to follow that step still, and if it is, be mindful not to chain more stitches than needed!

Your instruction for the second row might look like this:

"Row 2: 1ch, 2sc in 1 sc, 1 ch, skip 1 sc, repeat."

This would mean that, at the beginning of the row, you need to chain one, turn, and then do two single crochet into the bottom single crochet, chain one, skip one single

crochet from the bottom row, do another two single crochets into the next loop, and then proceed until the end of the row. The instructions for each row typically finish with ", turn." Patterns also slightly differ by whether they instruct to do the chain-one at the end of the first or the beginning of the second or each next row. Although this is technically irrelevant, you should still follow the pattern as a beginner to avoid confusion.

Tall Stitches

Tall stitches can be found in treble and triple crochet, and other taller stitches. Keep in mind that the treble is accounted for each time you turn a chain. When you're starting a new row, skip the bottom row's first stitch while turning chains.

Other Symbols

Crochet patterns typically include other symbols, like different brackets and asterisks as well as dashes, to further explain what you need to crochet in the particular row. These symbols mean several different things:

- Brackets, [ ], tell you how many times you should repeat a particular instruction. The set of brackets contains the instructions given inside with a number of repetitions given after it. For example: "[2ch, 2htc, 1 skip) 3 times]" means that you should chain two loops, do two half treble crochets, skip one loop, and repeat that sequence three times.

- Asterisks indicate that something should be repeated, and they're placed in front of the chain number (e.g. sc, *3tc, 2ch). Sometimes, you'll find them at the end of the instruction (e.g. "* to the end"), which means that the previously mentioned sequence should be repeated until the end of the row.

- Parentheses are used when several stitches are done in a single bottom stitch. For example, 2htc (3 dc, 1ch in next sc) would mean that you need to do two half-treble crochets and then work three treble crochet into the single crochet from the bottom row that's next to the one above which you did the half-treble crochets. Stitches like these sometimes create shell-like shapes, and other times, they look like popcorn or squares. Each of the sequences that are typical for a stand-out stitch look different, and you'll be able to memorize it with time.

Symbols like these are useful to simplify the pattern and make it easier for the artist to understand. However, there are still parts of doing crochet that remain a bit confusing to beginners for a while. When the instruction says "skip 1," confusion can occur about what it means. Skipping spaces usually refers to skipping particular chain arches from the previous row. However, a chain space means making a hole-like shape in your work by doing one of the taller chains, then skipping one or several chain loops, and then doing a single or double crochet into the designated chain of the selected stitch. Spaces can consist of one or multiple different-sized chains, which gives them a different shape. Spaces can be triangular, round, squared, and many other interesting shapes. However, when a space consists of three or more chains, it's called a loop (lp).

Now, let's discuss working in rounds in greater detail. Working in rounds isn't at all difficult but might appear so due to the complex look of the work. Creating round crochet pieces for flower motifs and granny squares begins with a loop chain. A looped chain, as mentioned earlier, is a base chain that consists of anywhere from a couple (three to five) to over 10 stitches. But when you reach the end of your chain, you don't turn over the work and chain one but instead pull the hook through the first loop of the chain. This creates a circular shape for working rounds. Your first round now begins as stated on the pattern, for example "(1ch, 1tc)* to the end, turn."

Loops

Your first, base chain is the basis for the entire work. But the remainder of your rows or rounds is done by weaving the yarn into the loops of the previous row. Yet when you look at the work, you'll notice that several different loops can be used. So how do you decide? Crochet patterns usually instruct crocheting into the 'front' or 'back' loop when relevant. In this case, the loop that is the closest to you is going to be the front, and the furthest one from you would be the back loop.

Garment Terminology

Believe it or not, making crochet clothing isn't very complicated either. However, you need to learn some of the basic terms that are used in garment patterns to fully enjoy the experience of making your sweaters, tops, skirts, and dresses. Terms like right/left front or back, shoulder, or sleeve mean the parts of the garment that match the part of the body it covers. The 'right' side of the garment is seen while wearing it, while the 'wrong' side is worn on the inside.

When you finish making different pieces of a sleeve, the instruction may prompt you to join them on the left- or right-hand corner, which means the corner that's closest to your hand. Doing the opposite side-piece would mean a bit more trouble for beginners. The instructions on the pattern will likely be given for one side, and you'll simply be told to reverse them for the other.

chapter 2
Must Have Crochet Supplies

Now that you know the basics of reading crochet patterns, it's time to start gathering your supplies.

Why is the Crochet Supply Selection so Important?

Your choices of supplies will affect comfort while working, speed, efficiency, and of course the beauty and quality of your work. While it's not necessary to have super expensive supplies, the knowledge about their different types, sizes, and best uses can make a difference between feeling confident and happy with your skills and facing obstacles and feeling like you're failing. I can't stress enough how important it is that you set yourself up for success with crochet or else you might want to quit before you even gave your talent a decent shot.

Crochet can be simple and wonderful to learn for beginners, even with more complex projects, so long as you're willing to make it easier for yourself with planning, strategizing, and choosing the most fitting tools. Now, what dictates the proper choice of tools?

- **Your personal preference.** No matter the quality of supplies, your hand will be the one to hold the hook and yarn. It's likely that you'll want to crochet for hours at a time, and even longer once you get a hold of the techniques. When crocheting for longer hours, you will feel the texture of the hook and yarn, the shape of your tool; its every bump, curve, and the edge will affect how comfortable you are. If you choose the wrong tools and materials, you might start to feel the tension in your hands or even injure your fingers over time. When this happens, it isn't because crochet isn't for you. It's because you have unique needs and preferences. For example, I know women who have long, elastic fingers and don't cope well with large, hard hooks. In this case, it's better to choose more modern, flexible hooks or wire hooks that don't cause too much stress. Similarly, there are ladies out there with strong hands and larger fingers who don't feel like they have enough control over small, thin hooks. In this case, it's better to choose a brand with a thicker handle that gives you more control, independent of the actual hook size. I could go on and on about the details that affect comfort while crocheting, but I'll leave you with this: The hook and yarn size aren't the only factors to consider. Yarn can be harder or softer in all sizes, and hooks come with different shapes and styles, all of which deserve a bit of experimentation before you commit to a more expensive tool or kit.

- **The type of work you want to do.** It's not the same if you wish to crochet simple blankets and covers and if you want to create intricate, unique pieces of clothing. Different crochet items dictate the hook yarn selection. For example, very few people are happy with using silk yarn for blankets and covers because it's a sleek, thin material. Instead, they wish to use chunkier, softer, fuzzy yarn that will give the right texture and warmth. Conversely, if you wish to make intricate summer dresses, it's less likely that you'll need supplies of soft woven yarn. Do a little bit of research about what materials are best for the type of work you're interested in making.

- **Your aesthetic.** Your preferred color scheme, desired stitching, and most com-

fortable textures all affect the type of tools and yarn that you should use. Unlike brand comparisons, which measure prices, quality, and magnitude of the offering side-by-side, you can also find numerous comparisons and reviews that lay out the best yarns and hooks for particular styles, stitches, sizes, and textures.

With that in mind, the following sections will give you a guide for choosing the most suitable beginner basic crochet supplies:

- Yarn

- Hooks

- Add-ons

- Organizers

Step #1: Best Yarn Selection

While there's not much difference between knitting and crochet yarn, beginners should learn about several traits of yarn that affect the right selection.

Weight

Crochet yarn comes in different weights that translate to the thickness of the yarn and the size, bulkiness, and elasticity of the final product. The yarn weight is printed on the label, and the labels usually indicate the recommended hook size for the particular yarn. I recommend for beginners to follow these instructions since they ensure a satisfying result. Once you're more experienced with crochet, you can start experimenting with different yarn-hook combos for interesting effects.

Yarn weight also concerns the matter of gauge or texture. The lighter the yarn, the greater number of stitches and motifs needed for a sample size. Conversely, thicker yarn will require fewer stitches and motifs for a comparable size. Another thing to factor in is that the combination of the yarn and hook affects the density and stitch size. For example, a smaller hook with chunky yarn will produce tight, thick fabric, while a larger hook with lighter weight yarn produces a stretched-out, drapery-looking fabric.

When making pieces of different sizes, you can achieve volume in two different ways. You can either use the same number of stitches with heavier yarn, or you can increase the number of stitches using a smaller yarn. You might end up with a same, or similar, enlarged size, but the appearance of the stitches and the scale of motifs will be different. For example, if you enlarge a granny square blanket using thicker yarn, you will get a larger blanket with the same number of squares, albeit larger, compared to the sample. But if you decide to, instead, use lighter yarn, you will get a bigger blanket with more granny squares compared to the sample. When you put two pieces next to one another, you will get a completely different result despite using the same size and stitches. The first blanket will likely be chunkier and thicker, while the latter will be lighter with more motifs. As you can see, the choice of yarn here dictates the results, so the decision should fall on the texture and thickness that you want.

Yarn weights indicate different levels of thickness with lightest being lace weight, which is fine and thin, and thickest being the 'roving' yarn weight. Slightly thicker than lace is the fingering weight, which is often considered to be a reference "happy middle" for beginners, while sport weight, DK, and worsted weight fall in the category of thicker yarns that are used for bulkier items. Each of the weights has its specific metrics or sizes. These sizes are written down on the pattern as recommended either by project or, if given, within a size chart. Here's a list of yarn sizes as a reference for purchasing with tension or gauge suggestions:

- Lace/weight yarn usually carries the size 16 plus label, requires around eight to nine stitches or loops for an inch, and requires around 35 wraps per inch (WPI) for tight tension.

- The fingering weight yarn is marked as size one to three and takes seven to eight stitches for an inch.

- Sport weight yarn carries sizes three to six, takes five to six stitches for an inch, and has 15-18 WPI tension.

- Light-worsted yarn, or DK, is considered to be the size five to seven, and takes five to six stitches for an inch.

- Bulky/Super bulky yarn is sized 9-11 on the label, needs four to five stitches for an inch, and has a 9-11 WPI.

- Super-bulky yarn is usually labeled as size 13-15 and counts 3-4 loops or stitches for an inch. Tight tension requires seven to eight wraps per inch.

Fiber

Choosing the type of fiber that you wish to use for crochet is one of the most important beginner decisions. You can choose between a variety of materials that are available on the market from natural wool to acrylic and cotton. Whichever choice you make, there will be some advantages and drawbacks that go with a particular type of yarn. Here are the most common fiber types:

- **Cotton.** If you wish to crochet items that need to endure wear and tear like cloths, rugs, and covers, or light items that can be worn during spring and summer like tops, dresses, and skirts, cotton yarn will be a great choice. It is light, breathable, and won't shrink or damage as easily as wool and other materials. Cotton yarn is also a great option if you want to make toys, covers, bags, and jewelry because it's thicker compared to wool and will maintain shape well. However, cotton isn't as elastic and easy to work with as wool would be. It won't stretch, so you'll have to pay extra attention to gauge or tension when crocheting.

- **Acrylic.** If you have an allergy to wool, or you don't want to use wool for numerous other reasons, you can always choose acrylic yarn. It's more affordable compared to natural wool and also comes in a variety of colors, designs, and textures. However, there are a couple of downsides to acrylic yarn. It's more heat-sensitive

22

than wool, so you won't be able to iron over it. Plus, acrylic threads are known to tear while crocheting, so extra caution with work will be required. Finally, acrylic yarn is more elastic compared to cotton but less compared to wool yarn. If you require additional elasticity or stretching abilities from your material, make sure to verify with the supplier whether or not, and to what degree, this yarn can be stretched out.

- **Wool.** This yarn is most popular in crochet overall, and it's particularly convenient for beginners. It has soft, firm fiber that covers mistakes well, and if you wish, you can always unravel it and repurpose the wool from the item that you no longer need. For those who are allergic to wool, there are always hypoallergenic options. With wool, you can play off of fiber thickness and texture to achieve a thinner or a chunkier look. If you want a large, heavy blanket, you don't have to necessarily use large amounts of wool. Instead, you can choose a chunky yarn that gives you more for less.

- **Thread.** Crochet thread is thicker yet lightweight, which is why many beginners opt for it while they're still learning. Thread is a better alternative to yarn if you want intricate, lacey works with more ornamental design than if you're going for utility and practicality. With that, you can choose between cotton, silk, and acrylic thread.

- **Maintenance.** Each yarn comes with different washing and maintenance instructions. Some yarns are machine washable and even resistant to dryers and high temperatures, while others only tolerate dry cleaning.

Special Considerations

There are several more specifications to consider when finding your perfect yarn. Texture can be smoother or chunkier, and many novelty yarns use sparkly or foiled threads for a more interesting effect. The color of the yarn is an important choice as well, and not just for taste and preference. I often advise beginners to start with lighter color yarns as they make it easier to see and count the stitches. The price of yarn can vary depending on the brand, but it doesn't necessarily have to correlate with quality. When deciding on the yarn, always compare the yardage measurements on the label. Despite one yarn being more expensive than the other, the difference may concern the quantity of the yarn more than quality. Likewise, when two yarns have the same price but a different yardage, it's indicative of either difference in quality or specifications. Yarn colors can be different from brand to brand and even across different batches of the same-brand yarn. Many beginners experience the frustration of buying the same yarn from two different sellers and in the same color, only to discover that even those colors don't match. Because of this, I recommend doing careful calculations concerning gauge and yardage and getting all the wool you need at once.

Furthermore, think about your preferred method of cleaning before purchasing the yarn so that you don't end up being disappointed later on. Finally, you can choose between natural and vegan wool. Here, 'vegan' doesn't only apply to cotton and acrylic yarn. Eco-friendly and animal rights-aware manufacturers make sure that no ani-

mal-based chemicals and dyes go into production so that there's the least bit of disruption to the environment included in your fine hobby. Organic yarn manufacturing, on the other hand, is dedicated to producing all-natural yarns that aren't processed with artificial chemicals and don't include non-organic dyes and fibers.

Step #2: Choose the Right Hook

When thinking about your hook selection, remember that there's no right or wrong hook. Each hook has the best-recommended uses, and of course, aligns with yarn weights. Before choosing your first hook, try a couple of different ones to see which one works the best with your stitches, and of course, how comfortable it is to hold each in your hand. The use of hooks will also vary depending on your project. Either way, beginners are most successful with basic crochet hooks, while specialty hooks tend to enter more confusion and, hence, do more harm than good. Keep this in mind as there are many different types of hooks to choose from for your crochet. Here are a couple of common hook types for recommendations usages:

- **Regular hooks.** Plain hooks that are friendly to beginners come in a variety of materials, shapes, and sizes. The medium-size (H-8, or 5mm) hook is considered a universal size and most beginner-friendly. It covers the biggest range of commonly used yarns and is suitable for a broad number of items like blankets, pillowcases, and clothing items. However, these hooks can be made from bamboo, metal, plastic, or aluminum, and each of these materials has unique benefits and downsides worth considering. For example, metal hooks are most available and durable. However, they can be hard on the hands and cause pain. Plastic hooks are at the lowest price point, which makes them the best option for anyone starting out and still searching for their hook of preference. It's also light and won't cause any pain while working. Bamboo hooks are popular because they keep stitches from slipping off, which is important when you're making chain spaces, complex stitches, and ornamental motifs. Once you're past the basic stitch stage, I recommend trying out bamboo hooks for some of your more intricate works. They'll prevent trouble with keeping several chains under control and hence prevent frustration and discouragement.

- **Afghan crochet hooks.** Afghan crochet is halfway between classic crochet and knitting, which is why these hooks are longer than normal crochet hooks. They are supposed to hold onto dozens of stitches for making thick, fabric-like rugs and blankets. If you're thinking of buying these hooks, keep in mind that you'll only be able to use them for the Tunisian stitch. Not that I have anything against this type of crochet, but it is a point to factor in, especially if you're looking to invest in higher-quality hooks.

- **Steel hooks.** Steel hooks are used to crochet fine items like doilies but usually don't work well with other types of crochet due to their size.

Beginner Hook Size Guide

Hooks come in too many types and sizes to count, so I'll suggest the best-recommended sizes to use with the most common yarn weights:

- Lace and thread yarn work best with No. 1-2 (1.5mm) and B-1 (2.25-2.5mm) hook.

- Superfine and fine yarns work best with C-2, D-3, E-4, and F-5 hooks. These hooks range between 2.75-3.75mm.

- Light worsted yarn works with 4-5.00 mm or G-6, No. 7, and H-8 hooks, while medium worsted yarn requires a 5.50-6.50 mm hook, mainly I-9, J-10, or K-11.

- Bulky yarn requires a 7-9mm hook, and you can choose between L, M, and N hooks, while super bulky yarn works best with 10-12mm hooks, marked with sizes N/M.

No matter the type of hook you choose, there are a couple more tips to keep in mind for more convenient use. First, it's important to point out that you should never change the hook size in the middle of the work. Even the smallest difference will show, and you will end up with something called a warped crochet. Of course, most crocheters experience frequent loss of hooks in the middle of work, often as they fall between cushions or simply roll underneath your couch. To avoid having to spend precious minutes rescuing your hooks, get several hooks of the same size and keep them next to you. That way, whenever your hook goes MIA, you can easily replace it with the same size hook. Next, remember to only slightly lubricate your hooks if you feel like the yarn isn't sliding as smoothly as you'd like. You can do this with a drop of oil or face/body lotion. Remember to polish the hook and then carefully wipe off the excess lubricant so that it doesn't stain your yarn. Also, remember to clean your hooks! Not only the lubricant but also oils from your fingers will stick onto your needle and eventually cause the icky-looking build-up of grease and tiny threads. This is neither comfortable nor nice to work with. Finally, organize your hooks by size so that you can find them easily.

Yarn and hooks aren't the only things needed for a successful crochet. In the next section, you'll find out what other add-ons and accessories will be useful for successful work.

Step #3: Decide on the Ideal Tools and Add-ons

While hooks and yarn are the basic condiments of gorgeous crochet, you will need a couple more tools for the sleek, hustle-free craft. Here's the list of additional tools and supplies that you will need:

Markers

I recommend all beginners use markers to highlight stitches while working with patterns. There are two ways to make your markers work for you while doing a new pattern. The first is to mark down the pattern size that you're working with in case you get a multi-size diagram. The second useful way would be to match your markers with yarn color—or assign colors to different yarn colors if you're working with neutrals—and section out the diagram and instructions. This can also apply to motifs and different

parts of the work, which will make the work appear a lot easier and more comfortable.

Scissors

I recommend getting a pair of fine scissors with smaller blades. You will need them to snip the yarn when you're starting and finishing a project. If you don't want to invest in specialty scissors, any pair will do just fine. Regardless of what scissors you choose, I advise you to set a pair aside for crochet only and keep them next to your other supplies. The last thing you need when you're about to start a project or switch yarns is to have to go around your house looking for a pair of scissors.

Darning Needles

You will need at least one darning needle when finishing the project. When you finish the last row or round, you need to snip off and weave the remaining yarn into the fabric. I recommend getting a set of darning needles that matches the yarns and hooks that you're using. This is because the needle's eye needs to be well adjusted to the thickness of the yarn.

A Ruler and a Tape Measure

Your crocheting kit should also feature two tools to measure lengths. You'll get good use of your ruler to check the work size in the middle of the project, while the tape measure helps keep a larger item's size in check.

A Pattern Collection

While I encourage trying out a variety of different crochet projects, it's also a good idea to collect patterns before you start working. This will help you plan out your work, how much yarn you need, what yarn to buy, and overall help you make a comprehensive schedule.

chapter 3
How to Crochet for Right Handers

N ow that you know what supplies you need for relaxing crochet, it's time to start learning the right techniques. Before you begin, I advise that you choose a simple pattern to start with, ideally one consisting of the same repeating stitch. In this chapter, you will learn how to crochet simple and chain stitches, which are the basis for other, more complex stitches. For starters, find the simplest pattern available, and choose the hook, yarn, scissors, and a needle that match the instructions given in the pattern. Once you've done that, it's time to start!

How to Hold the Hook and Yarn

The first important step is to find a way to hold your hook and yarn in ways that are most comfortable. I advise using your dominant hand. In this chapter, the advice will be given for crocheters whose dominant hand is right, but other than that, you can apply all the remaining advice for crocheting even if your dominant hand is left. Working with your dominant hand is important to prevent pain and cramping. I'd like to point out that your dominant hand isn't always the one that you hold your pencil with. There are many people who write with their right hand but hold knives, scissors, or do make-up with the opposite hand and vice versa! There's no right or wrong hand to crochet with, so just pick up the hook with one hand, hold it for a bit, and then pick it up with the other and simply decide which hand feels more comfortable and has better coordination and control over the hook.

Generally speaking, there are two basic ways to hold the hook and yarn. The first way, or position, is called "over-the-hook." With this position, your hand holds the hook like a pencil, with the handle resting on your palm. Your hand then goes over the hook, while your index finger and thumb grasp the indentation in the hook handle called the "thumb rest." With the second position, called "under-the-hook," you hold your hook like a spatula, with the hand and palm placed under it while your forefinger and thumb rest in the handle indentation.

Learning how to hold the yarn correctly is important so that you better control the tension which determines the size of your work. Beginners who don't yet know how to control tension often get frustrated because their work isn't turning out as intended. It's either crooked, too tight to the point of making crochet uncomfortable, too loose as to cause the yarn to slide off the hook, or their work turns out all the wrong size. Luckily for you, you don't have to go through months of frustrating failure to master control of your yarn and start making beautiful crochet. You can assume control over how much tension you apply so that your work always turns out accurate.

Now, this can be a very challenging first step. I advise you to set aside a couple of hours just to practice tension, which will, simultaneously, give you some of that precious, intuitive muscle memory that's needed for effortless, sleek stitches. The first time you start holding the hook and yarn might feel strange because you still don't have the proper muscle memory, not because you lack talent or skill. But why is muscle memory so important for crochet? Muscle memory consists of your brain memorizing the micromovements needed when doing crochet. Crochet can initially feel challenging because you have to focus intentionally on each little move. But with repetition, your hands and fingers form a sort of a natural feeling and flow of movement that becomes

automatic, hence being faster and more enjoyable. With practice, you will soon be able to march through rows and rounds of crochet without missing out on a single scene of your favorite show! Now, I imagine how exciting it felt as you imagined to finish reading this book and jump straight into making fine, intricate crochet. Instead, I implore you to be patient and run a couple of exercises first to set yourself up for success. Tension in crochet directly reflects the pressure you put on the yarn while you're using it by pulling it from your skein. You're looking for a "happy middle" that won't strain your hands as you work, and is neither too loose nor too tight. The way to discover this is by first checking if your natural, or intuitive stress/pressure is tight or loose.

To learn whether your natural tension is tight or loose, weave a strand of yarn between your pinky, ring, middle, and pointer finger. Tight tension will feel uncomfortable like your fingers are tied up in the strand, while loose tension will cause the strand to hang or fall off your fingers. The desired outcome is a secure, comfortable weave that stays in place.

Tight Tension

Tight tension happens when you pull too hard on the yarn while crocheting. Your work ends up being smaller compared to the sample. One of the best ways to tell if your tension is too tight is if you struggle to make a foundation chain. Your chain won't seem to have any gaps in the middle of loops, and it will be difficult to insert the hook beneath the loops since the threads are too tight. It will also be more difficult to pull the yarn through loops since you're tugging too hard through a too tight loop. If your tension is too tight, making a base chain might feel more like making a series of tight knots than a soft, comfy, crochet piece.

Loose Tension

If you naturally crochet with loose tension, your stitches will look crooked, your yarn will fall off the hook as you grab, and your swatch ends up being bigger than needed. Perhaps the easiest way to discover if your tension is loose is feeling like you're not in control of your work at all. While crocheting, the pressure of your hands might be too weak, so both your work and the hook and yarn feel like they'll drop any minute.

Grab Control of Your Tension!

Now, it's time to start finding a happy middle with yarn tension. If your natural tension is loose, you then need to start applying more pressure to your work. You can practice this by weaving the yarn between your pinky, ring, middle, and pointer finger. Weave the yarn over and over again until you achieve doing it without either having the yarn fall off your fingers or tightening around them.

The same exercise can be applied if your tension is tight as well. When you weave the yarn between fingers, tight tension will cause an uncomfortable tightening sensation. Practice reducing applied pressure until your weave is secure but comfortable.

Yarn Over

The next automatic, intuitive movement to learn is how to "yarn over." The yarn over is often spelled as 'YO' in beginner instruction, and it describes a movement of rolling the hook over or under a strand of yarn, pick it up with the hook, and pull through one of the chain loops, which then finishes the previous stitch and creates a loop for the next stitch. Yarn over is seemingly simple when you look at it in a video tutorial, but once you try doing it on your own, it becomes a bit trickier. In this section, you will learn a couple of instructions for how to yarn over in different situations and work stages.

The way you yarn over can affect your work result and of course make the process more or less comfortable. To "yarn over" means to ready your hands to start crocheting with your hook in the right and the yarn in the left hand. You should control the yarn with your index finger. Now, you need to bring your hook over the top of the strand, which places the yarn in front of the hook, in a low right to upper left direction. This is a simple movement that I still recommend exercising a couple of dozen times until it starts to feel natural.

When you're doing a single crochet stitch, which is the simplest stitch to use as a beginner, you first need to insert the hook into the gap beneath the stitch loop, pull the strand up with your hook, and then pull it through two of the remaining loops.

There is a different way of pulling a strand through a loop, and it's called "yarn under." This technique means working the strand underneath the chain stitch instead of over it. This creates an indentation in the work, which is done intentionally with some stitches. However, if you yarn under by accident, you can end up with uneven work that looks like it has a tiny hole in it. The yarn over gives the effect of parallel single crochets, while the yarn under creates an appearance of crossed single crochet. Pay attention to not alternate these techniques if not planned because this can affect the size and the appearance of your work.

Chain Stitch

This is it! It's time to start making your first crochet! Every crochet creation starts with a base chain. Making the base chain is also a great opportunity for you to check your tension. Remember to hold the yarn with moderate tension and to yarn over. These two things will greatly help in making a nice base chain.

A chain consists of chain stitches, and you begin this process by making a slip knot. All you have to do is wrap the strand around your hook to create a loop. You should see a shorter piece of the strand on one side of your hook and a longer piece that is connected to the ball of yarn. Now pick up the strand beneath the hook and pull it through the loop. Tighten the knot by pulling the yarn tail. Voila! You have a nice slip knot to start making your base chain!

Once you are pleased with your slip knot, hold the knot with your thumb and middle finger and guide the strand from the backside of the knot to the hook handle. Pull the strand through the hook's loop to form the first chain stitch. Repeat this process the

required number of times, and you have created a base chain. Keep in mind that your slip knot and the first chain won't count as stitches. Only start counting stitches once you've completed the first two steps.

The next step is to make a test swatch to learn if the tension that you make intuitively matches the pattern. We all have different levels of strength in your hands, so you might instinctively grasp the hook and yarn more or less firmly. There are no rules here, just your natural feeling. This step will coincide with making a crochet chain, or the base chain that we talked about in the first chapter of the book. If your pattern says to make a base chain out of an X number of stitches, do that and see if your swatch matches the measurements given in the pattern. You will do this by measuring the swatch with a ruler or a measuring tape. Most beginner patterns are 'small', which means that they number fewer chain stitches. If your pattern is larger, you don't have to make an entire chain. Instead, make the number of stitches that create a comparable size, e.g. one or five inches, which will make unraveling easier if your tension isn't right.

Upon making a swatch, compare it with the pattern to see if you've got the right tension. Perhaps you need to unravel, go back, and start over with more or less tension depending on the result. If your swatch is larger than the pattern sample, you need to start over with stronger tension. Conversely, you need to reduce tension and crochet more loosely in case your swatch was smaller compared to pattern measurements.

Magic Ring

Magic rings are the basis for many round, square, and rectangular crochets. They allow you to create numerous shapes by extending or reducing chains, as well as adding or reducing stitches as you crochet around a circle. You make a magic ring simply by chaining a desired number of stitches and then adding a slip stitch to the first stitch of the chain to close it and make a ring. After that, you can crochet a series of single crochets around these base stitches.

chapter 4

How to Crochet for Those with a Dominant Left Hand

But of course, not everyone's right hand is their dominant hand. Those with a dominant left hand can rest assured because crochet has a place for them too. Though there are not many changes, there are a few fundamental switches that are needed for maximum comfort and ease of use.

The Hook Should be in Your Left Hand

One major 'difference' with left-hand crochet is that the direction of your work changes. Right-handed crocheters work left-to-right while left-handers work right-to-left. This can make reading patterns and watching tutorials confusing. Remember, so long as you follow the same described steps, there will be no differences to your work. To better control the yarn and hooks, left-handers should hold the hook in their left hand and yarn in the right.

Chaining

Chaining is also the same with the left as it would be with the right hand. You need to pick up the yarn with your right and hook with the left hand and proceed to yarn over and pull through with your left hand until you've made a desired number of chains.

Slip Stitching

To do a slip stitch, use the right hand to insert the hook into a loop and then yarn over and pull through. It's as easy as that!

Crocheting in Circle

When making a magic circle with your right hand, hold the yarn in the right hand. Make a loop with your fingers and then, with the hook in the left hand, insert the tool into the loop, yarn over, and pull through. This will begin a chain for your magic ring, that you then close by slip stitching into the initial stitch and proceeding to make single crochets right to left.

34

chapter 5

Before You Start
— Crochet Beginner Tips —

Aside from getting the right supplies, you also need to sort and store your supplies appropriately to enjoy comfortable work. If your supplies are scattered all over the place, the work will feel chaotic, and you'll feel less inclined to crochet over time. But if your supplies are neatly sorted out, you'll feel happy and excited whenever you want to work, which will further motivate you to keep going. When it comes to organizing crochet supplies, there are only a couple of simple rules that you need to follow for seamless work:

Tip #1: Mind the Yarn

Above all else, it's necessary to take proper care of your yarn for a successful and enjoyable crochet. In the previous section, I recommended getting all of your yarn for a single crochet project at once to avoid notable differences in color. Once you begin with crochet, you will soon learn that yarn isn't as expensive as it looks, if you choose fancier options. In fact, many people choose to stock up on their favorite yarns so that it doesn't run out. But what is the best way to store these yarns? There are several ways to do it that depend on the types of projects that you're doing. Think about your projects and how you'll use the yarn before deciding how to sort it. Here are a couple of suggestions:

- **By color.** You can keep the same or similar colored yarns in the same bag or container, which is particularly important if you're working with several projects at once.

- **By size.** Once you collect substantial amounts of yarn, it might happen that you mix up sizes. This isn't good! Whenever you have several different yarn thicknesses at your workstation, keep them separate.

- **By project.** If you're making complex pieces that include several different yarn types or colors, you can also organize them by the project. For example, you can store them in bins and baskets labeled 'pillowcases' and 'blankets' so that you don't get confused.

- **By type.** If you need your machine-washable yarn strictly for your blankets and dresses, while clothes and rugs can be done well with acrylic yarns, and your bed covers deserve lush, high-quality organic yarn. You can also keep yarns separated by type. This will ensure that all of your items are done with materials that have the necessary traits and qualities.

- **By use.** I recommend keeping yarns separate in regards to their intended purpose. For example, if you planned on using some yarns during the week, and set some others aside for next week or the next months, you can also store them in a separate container and label them.

Tip #2: Sort Tools Out

Whether it's scissors, needles, yarn, or hooks, items need to be sorted out so that you can find them easily. The best way to ensure that your work supplies are orderly is to

take them out at least once a week and separate them by top, color, size, use, or any other applicable criteria.

Tip #3: Design Your Workstation

The layout of your craft room and workstation depends on your activities and preferences. Overall, I recommend having different areas or stations for yarns, hooks, accessories, and patterns. I also advise keeping a basket or a bin of supplies that you need while working close to you, and this bin should include spare hooks, a needle, scissors, and ongoing patterns. Whether you've dedicated an entire room to crochet, or only a single shelf in your dresser, having separate organizers, shelves, or drawers for different supplies is a great idea. The last thing you need is to have needles and scissors get stuck in your yarn while you're trying to work!

Tip #4: Get the Right Organizers

There are several types of organizers that you can use for tools and supplies. Baskets, bins, plastic containers, ziplock bags, and any other boxes and bags are great containers so long as they're big enough to fit your supplies. Once you've sorted them all out, place your supplies in appropriate containers.

Another option is to get drawer separators and organizers. Spring-loaded separator drawers are great not just for clothes but for sectioning out drawers to keep your yarns and tools from getting tangled together. You can also use pocket organizers that section out small pockets of the drawers for socks and undergarments. Instead, separate your yarns into the pockets to keep them from mixing while still being able to see all the colors.

Tip #5: Label Everything!

You might think that you know all of the colors, sizes, and weights by heart, but think again! Amid rushing to start your work, you might forget which of your yarns go with which hooks, which can cause uncomfortable confusion. Get adhesive label stickers or a label maker, and markdown everything you can. The more supplies you have, the more important it is to stay on track with your labels. Write down what each of the containers have inside, including types, colors, and sizes.

Tip #6: Print Out a Map and a Schedule

Finally, create a map of your workstation or craft room as a reminder of which area is designated for different supplies, and where each item should go. Print out the map, frame it, and keep it somewhere close so that you never get confused!

chapter 6
Crochet Pattern Techniques

Now that we're a little more comfortable with some of the basics, let's talk about some things you might come across in terms of techniques and vocabulary. There are a few stitch names that are interchangeable depending on where the pattern comes from, what country you live in, and sometimes preference between the two. Below are some of the terms that can be used interchangeably so that when you come across this new vocabulary, you won't be caught off guard!

Single Crochet

Depending on the literature that you're using, you might come across terms like single crochet. Keep in mind that these terms are interchangeable, and this one simply means the shortest and simplest crochet stitch. Single crochet is the easiest stitch that you can use for any crochet item that you want to make. All you need to do is start with a base chain and work your rows in the following pattern:

1. Hook into the first chain of your base. Upon making the base chain, the first stitch to add the hook into would be the first one from your hook.

2. Draw up one loop to create two loops on the hook. To "draw up" means to pick up the strand with the hook and pull it through the stitch. Here, you need to be extra careful with tension. Make sure not to squeeze the strand too tightly between your middle and pointer finger. Single crochet is a tiny stitch, and you might feel as if holding the yarn tightly increases your precision, but this is wrong. If you feel like you have to tug on the strand with the hook just to pull it through, your tension is too tight.

3. Then, you need to yarn over again and pull the strand through all of the loops until you're left with a single loop on your hook.

4. Skipping one chain from your base or the bottom row will create a chain space. If you go straight into making another single crochet, you will reduce the gauge and shorten your sample. This 'move' is often used when making asymmetrical shapes. If you want to preserve the same length, you need to chain one to bridge the gap between single crochets and then proceed with working the next chain.

Double Crochet

While single crochet results in a thicker, more knit-looking fabric, double crochet gives your material a looser, drapier look. It is a taller stitch compared to the single, and a row of the same yarn done in a double crochet will be twice the height of the single crochet. This is important to remember when planning your piece. As all stitches, it needs a base chain, and is done in following steps:

1. Yarn over and hook into the first chain gap next to your hook.

2. Yarn over again, pull one loop up by picking it up with the hook. Mind the tension and release the yarn a bit if you start tugging on it.

3. Pull the yarn through two loops on your hook.

4. Yarn over again and pull through all of the loops.

The double crochet is a one of the base stitches for making more intricate patterns like the shell stitch, the bean stitch, the diamond stitch, and others. The effect of different shapes is achieved with combinations of single single and double crochet. As with the single crochet, skipping one base or bottom row chain will create a gap in the fabric. If you don't want to bring down the pattern, you need to chain one to maintain the same gauge. As with the single crochet, you can make any piece you want using this single stitch, if you consider that there will be visible gaps in the fabric.

Half Double (US)/Treble Crochet

If you can't make up your mind between the thick single and the drapey double crochet, there is a happy middle! The half-double crochet gives you the best of both worlds. The stitch can be used for all materials and items because it gives enough thickness and consistency for utilitarian value (e.g. a pair of socks or a blanket that will truly keep you warm), while maintaining the ornamental, hand-made appeal of traditional crochet. Here's the traditional way of doing the 'HDC':

1. Chain two after finishing your base chain. Unlike the single crochet, the second added chain results in more height.

2. Like with the double crochet, you now need to yarn over before inserting the hook into the next chain space.

3. Yarn over once more and pull one loop up, and you now have three loops on your hook.

4. Yarn over again to create the fourth loop, and pool through all of the loops.

You now have your first half-double crochet stitch. It will result in taller rows compared to single crochet and lower rows compared to the double crochet; also, you may notice that the spaces between the chains are slightly more condensed. This stitch can also be used to make other complex stitches when you want to make them more condensed and less lacey. However, a more ornamental look will still require taller stitches like double or triple crochets.

Triple(US)/Treble(UK) Crochet

The triple crochet is the tallest stitch of the bunch. When making it from the base chain, you need to create a chain-four as your turning chain and begin with your triple crochet:

1. Yarn over twice instead of once. This will create an additional loop for your hook and extend the chain.

2. Insert the hook into the base chain's fifth chain, yarn over again, and pull the yarn through the stitch. You will now have four loops on the hook. Yarn over again to create the fifth, and pull the strand through the first two loops.

3. Yarn over again and pull the yarn through the remaining two loops.

4. After creating your first triple crochet, you should do the next one by yarning over twice and inserting the hook into the next chain.

As you can see, there's nothing difficult about different basic crochet stitches. Starting from the simplest single crochet, the number of times that you yarn over and whether you pull through two or all the loops once decides the length of your chain. The longer you practice these different stitches, the more automatic and intuitive your movements become. I recommend creating a square featuring different crochet stitch swatches from your favorite yarns. If you're particularly attached to a certain yarn type or size, doing this will give you gauge references that you can use when deciding on the stitching for your next piece.

44

chapter 7
Easy and Fun Crochet Patterns for Beginners

T he following are just a few patterns that you can start immediately! We will go through step-by-step how to start each pattern as well as suggested materials and yarn types. For beginners, it's best to follow the suggestions for materials until you get the hang of things. If you wish to branch out and experiment, just remember to have fun while doing so!

Pattern #1: Your Cute Washcloth

It's time to make your first crochet art piece! Washcloths are great first project ideas. You can make them in a variety of colors and yarns, and they always make beautiful decorations and presents. Here's how to make them:

- **Supplies:**
    - Worsted yarn in the color that you like
    - A pair of scissors
    - Hook, size K
    - One needle

- **Instructions:**
    - Make a 19-stitch base chain.
    - Chain one and turn.
    - Make the first row using single crochets.
    - Repeat until you make the desired size.

○ Cut and tie off extra yarn when you're done.

○ Weave in the remaining strand.

Pattern #2: A Colorful Pique Towel

Whether for your kitchen or your bathroom, this pique-stitch towel will make a perfect addition to your colorful samples! You will use one new stitch, and it's called a pique stitch. The gauge for this piece will be about 24 stitches for 28 rows, which will equal eight inches or 20 centimeters. Your finished piece should measure 21in by 36in, or 53 by 92 centimeters. If you wish to reduce or increase the size, do so proportionally since it takes three stitches for an inch of fabric. Now, let's get to learning new stitches and techniques!

- **Supplies:**

  - ○ Three balls of yarn of 100g (2x5) with each being a different color

  - ○ One ball of 100g yarn in a neutral color. To better coordinate colors, I recommend getting either three different shades of the same color, or a light-to-medium and dark shade of one color with a dark shade of another, complementary color.

- **Instructions:**

  - ○ Chain 64, then chain one and turn.

  - ○ Work 60 pique stitches by starting at the 3rd chain from your hook. Here's how to make a pique stitch:

    - ■ Yarn over and hook into the third chain from the beginning of the row.

    - ■ Yarn over, draw up one loop. You now have three loops on your hook.

    - ■ Yarn over again and draw your hook through two loops.

    - ■ Yarn over and hook into the base stitch that you already worked in, draw up one loop to make four loops on the hook.

    - ■ Yarn over and pull the strand through all of the loops.

○ When you get to the end of the row, chain one and turn.

○ Work a second row with single crochets into each stitch.

○ When you get to the end, chain one and turn.

○ Proceed alternating rows of pique stitch and single stitches until you complete your towel.

○ Switch colors at the fifth row, and proceed changing colors every two rows (after you make one pique and one single stitch row).

Pattern #3: The Simplest Blanket

Whether you choose to make a baby blanket or a queen-size, lush cover, this simple stitch crochet will give you hours of relaxing fun with little to no mental and physical strain. Plus, it's easy to vary yarn, textures, and colors any way you please! On average, it will take you about a day to make a baby blanket size, while larger sizes will take a couple of days.

● **Supplies:**

○ Light worsted yarn

○ A hook

○ One needle

- ◯ A pair of scissors
- ◯ Measuring tape

- ● **Instructions:**
  - ◯ Write down customized measurements for your blanket.
  - ◯ Make a base chain in the desired length, which you'll verify by measuring with the tape.
  - ◯ Proceed with single crochets until you reach the end of the row.
  - ◯ Chain one, turn.
  - ◯ Proceed with a desired number of rows until you reach the targeted size.

Pattern #4: A Unisex Scarf

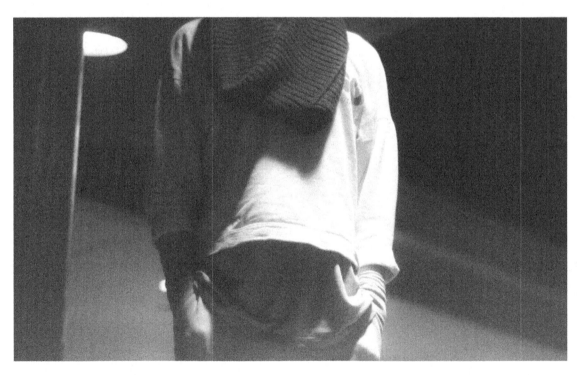

Choose a neutral-color yarn, and your comfy hand-made scarfs become a delight for the entire family! The fabric that you're about to make will resemble knitting yet require a lot less work. Your scarf will measure five by 75 inches and will require 16 stitches for four inches or 10 cm, in case you wish to alter the dimensions. Here's what you need for to make your unisex scarf:

- **Supplies:**
  - Light worsted yarn, 500 yards
  - One needle
  - A K (6.5mm) hook
  - A pair of scissors

- **Instructions:**
  - Chain a 301 stitch.
  - Add a slip stitch to your second chain from the hook, and proceed for another 300 stitches for the entire first and second row.
  - For the third row, add a slip stitch into each bottom stitch.
  - In the fourth row, add a slip stitch to each front loop in the bottom row, and repeat for the fifth and sixth row.
  - Turn the work, and proceed adding slip stitches into each row until you achieve the desired size.
  - Don't forget to turn over the work after each row to make the distinct pattern!

Pattern #5: Women's Infinity Scarf

How about an elegant yet soft and practical infinity scarf? If you haven't yet made one of those before, it's time to learn! The best thing about this pattern is that it's done with a single, repetitive stitch that will help you unwind after a hard working day.

- **Supplies:**

    - Bulky yarn, one skein
    - A size Q hook
    - One needle
    - A pair of scissors

- **Instructions:**

    - Chain 62 base stitches.
    - For the first row, add a half-double crochet into each bottom chain stitch.
    - Repeat half-double crochet stitches for the remaining rows.
    - Tie off the strand once you've completed the desired size of the scarf.
    - Sew the two ends of the scarf together.

Optionally, if you wish to make a larger size, you can twist the infinity scarf once or twice, and sew in the joints so that it maintains the twisted shape.

chapter 8
Crochet Stitches
— Beginner and Specialty —

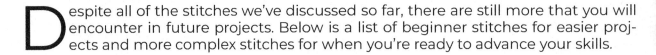

Despite all of the stitches we've discussed so far, there are still more that you will encounter in future projects. Below is a list of beginner stitches for easier projects and more complex stitches for when you're ready to advance your skills.

Beginner Stitches

The following stitches are just a few that you will encounter in some beginner projects. We'll talk about where they work best and how to stitch them.

1. Moss Stitch

The moss stitch resembles a thick net. It's interesting and universal since it's consistent and repetitive, but it doesn't have the visible line patterns that are typical for crochet. As such, you can use it when you want a soft, knit-looking fabric that has minimum gaps. Here's how to make a moss stitch:

- Make a base chain, turn over, and then add a single crochet to the third chain from the beginning until the end of the first row.

- Add single crochets into the each following space (gap) of the bottom single crochet.

- Remember: Don't crochet into the top chain stitches of bottom rows, but instead into chain *spaces*. That's how you'll close off the gaps and get the desired thickness of the fabric.

2. The Shell Stitch

With a complete base chain, then continuing with the following:

- Add a single crochet to the chain's second stitch.

- Skip two and add a double crochet to the third chain stitch.

- Add another four double crochets to the same stitch so that you have five of them.

- Do a single crochet into the next stitch, chain one, skip two chains.

- Make five double crochets, skip two, and add a single crochet to the following chain.

- This will be your second shell, and you can make as many as you want!

3. Single-Crochet Front Loop

If you want a lacey-looking pattern that's still very consistent and fabric-like, then this stitch will work wonders for you! Start off with a base chain and proceed with the following:

- Work a row of single-crochets.

- Add three rows of front-loop single crochets.

- Alternate to another row of single crochets.

- Repeat until you've made the desired size.

- Achieve greater contrast by alternating lighter and heavier yarns for single and front-loops single crochet, so long as their use is consistent.

4. Treble Shell

If you want larger, more distinct shells, then simply use treble instead of single cro-

chets! It's as simple as that. Here are the altered instructions:

- Add a half-double crochet at the beginning of the row instead of the single crochet.

- Skip three chain stitches instead of two.

- Close off shells with a half-double instead of the single crochet.

5. Mesh Stitch

The mesh stitch is similar to the moss stitch, except it shows visible gaps while still being thick and consistent. Make a base chain and do the following:

- Add a single crochet to the base's third chain.

- Skip a chain and add a single crochet into the next base or bottom chain.

- Finish the row, turn, and repeat for as long as needed.

Specialty Stitches

You'll want to expand your talents to more advanced stuff, and that's fantastic! But with complex projects comes specialty stitches. Here are some common speciality stitches that can show up in projects you wish to take on.

1. Diamond Stitch

This adorable stitch creates a waffle-like fabric. It's heavier in appearance, and it will be a great option if you want a fabric with a strong texture and firm consistency. Add the following crochets to your base chain:

- Start your first row by adding a single crochet to the second chain from the beginning. Finish the row with a single crochet.

- Chain three and a double crochet to each stitch until the end of the row.

- To start the third row, chain one and add a front-post-treble-crochet to the first row's single crochet's chain.

- Skip one stitch next to the one you worked in and do a single crochet, then another front-post into the fourth stitch. This would be the same chain that you worked your first front-post into.

- Repeat until you reach the final two stitches in the row. Add a front-post to the same single crochet where the previous front-post was, and finish the last stitch with a single crochet.

- Chain one and turn, starting another row, yarn over twice and hook into the closest single crochet. Proceed with a treble, and continue as instructed at the beginning.

2. Lacy Treble Shell

Even better than the shell stitch is a light, breathable version that you'll love to use with your summer creations. Upon chaining a desired number for the base, follow the repeating pattern:

- Treble crochet, chain one, treble, chain one, treble, chain one, treble.

- Close the shell with a half-double crochet into the next free stitch and start making other shells.

- To begin a next-row shell, chain four instead of three, like you did with the regular treble shell.

3. Bean Stitch

The bean stitch is only slightly different from the puff stitch, which we'll look at in just a bit. While there are many similarities in the fabric, it has a little bit more of a geometric shape with a tad more visible spaces. After chaining as many odd-number stitches as you want, continue with this pattern:

- Hook into the third chain, pull up to have two loops on your hook, and continue to hook into the same stitch and pull up until you have a total of six loops.

- Yarn over and pull through the six loops, and then seal the stitch with a chain-one.

- Skip a chain, and create another bean in the next stitch. Proceed to make little beans until you complete a row, and then chain one after finishing the last bean to begin the next row.

- After you've turned the work, skip one stitch and start working into the next one.

4. The V-Stitch

This simple stitch gives your fabric an intricate, geometric appeal albeit with little fuss. All you need to do after making the base chain is to follow these steps:

- Make one double crochet into the bottom chain or row space, not stitch.

- Add one chain stitch to the same space, and top it with another single crochet in the same space.

- Chain one and go along the base until you finish!

5. The Puff Stitch

This fun stitch will produce a bubbly-looking fabric, which will feel warm and soft against the skin. Upon making a base chain, chain one and continue with these steps:

- Place the hook into the bottom row stitch, hook the strand, pull through, yarn over, and hook into the same stitch, pull a strand through, and repeat five more times.

- With seven loops hooked on, yarn over once more and pull the strand through all of the loops.

Chain one and repeat until you complete the work!

chapter 9

Simple Crochet Projects for Every Season

N ow that we've looked at and practiced some stitches, it's finally time to start creating projects of your own! Feel free to repeat or experiment with any of these projects. Create what you want, and try as many as you like!

Blankets and Throws

Beginner Baby Blanket

To start, you will be making a plain and simple baby blanket with a single crochet across all the rows of your work. The best thing about this pattern is that you can alter the sizing and use the same principle to make blankets, covers, and throws in different sizes and textures. This pattern will apply to size four yarn.

Supplies

- Size four yarn in the color that you like, approx. 1,006 yards.
- Scissors
- A 4.5 mm hook
- Needle

Instructions

- Chain 15 stitches; chain one and turn over the work.

- Begin the second row with a single crochet.

- Complete another 14 rows; fasten off and weave in the remaining strand with the needle.

Drapey Double-Crochet Throw

The appeal of this blanket will be achieved by varying colors of the yarn and introducing square gaps that will add to the intricate look of the fabric.

Supplies:

- A measuring tape

- Three different size three yarns, approx 5,000 yards (1,500-2,000 yards per color)

- A size H hook

- A needle and a pair of scissors

Instructions:

- Make the blanket using the "rule of fours": Chain as many stitches for your base chain as needed to complete your measure.

- Crochet four double-crochet rows in a single color and then stitch colors at the end of the row.

- For the fifth row, start with four double crochets and then skip another four to

create a gap.

- Bridge the gap by chaining four and adding a double crochet into the fifth stitch from the ones you skipped.

- Crochet another three rows in the same color, switch to a third color, and repeat the pattern.

- Proceed until you complete the desired size!

Drapey Triple Crochet Rug

Rugs are among the most practicable crochet creations to make. They're otherwise quite costly to buy, and you can make yours from finest yarns for a fraction of the price. Plus, you get to be as creative as you want and fully customize the colors to your home! Here's what you'll need:

Supplies:

- Acrylic chunky yarn, 1,500-2,000 yards, one or multiple colors

- A measuring tape

- A matching hook

- A needle and a pair of scissors

Instructions:

- Choose a size and make your base chain. Measure with the tape to confirm that you have enough chain stitches.

- Depending on your size, make between five and ten rows with triple crochet before alternating the colors.

- Switch to a different color and make five rows of triple crochet.

- Switch to your previous color and make five more rows with triple crochet.

- Measure with the tape to see how much length from your final piece should go for alternating colors and how much should go into the middle section.

- Go back to your first color and work the middle section of the blanket.

- Finish the blanket by alternating the final colors the same way as you started: five rows in the contrasting color, five in the main, and five in the contrasting color.

Pillows

Easy Crochet Pillow

There are few things as simple as making crochet pillowcases. All you need to do is follow these few rules:

- Choose your pillow. Take its measurements, add an inch for each side, and you have the measurements for your sample shape!

- Your crochet pillowcase will consist of two same-shape pieces that you'll first make and then sew together at three sides so that you can insert the pillow at the fourth.

- Make the bottom side of your sample the measurement for the chain base.

- Choose the yarn, hook, and stitch. The first choice falls on the type of yarn, which will dictate the gauge. Then, choose the stitch. You can do a plain single, double, or triple crochet, or go for one of the specialty stitches from chapter eight.

- Make your swatch. Your swatch will consist of the measured base chain and the first row made with your selected stitch. If your sample matches the size of your pillow (there should be about an inch of space on each side), proceed making a desired number of rows.

- Your piece should be two inches taller than the sample pillow.

- Proceed finishing one side of the pillowcase by crocheting the right number of rows.

- Repeat the same steps for the back side of the pillow, and sew the two parts to-

gether.

Here are some ideas for creative crochet pillows that you can apply to all sizes, yarns, and stitches:

Single Crochet Pillow

In this image, you can see a plain crochet pillowcase made with size three yarn. It features a cute, woven, fall-themed application. You can vary your colors and applications for a unique result.

Comfy Double Crochet Pillow

Using the same principles, you can make double-crochet pillowcases in a variety of colors and shapes. You can then add woven decorations, pompoms, and other add-ons to make a unique-looking pillow.

Shawls

Simple Crochet Shawl

Supplies:

- Two different size three yarns, 250 yards of each color

- One 5.5mm hook

- A pair of scissors and a needle

Instructions:

- Your gauge will be six stitches by four rows for a shawl of 58 by 24 inches.

- Create a magic circle. Make the first round by chaining three, making three double crochets, then chain two, and finishing with four double crochets.

- For the third round, chain three and add a double crochet to the first stitch. Make a double crochet and add a pattern (double crochet, chain two, double crochet) to the second chain slip stitch in the bottom row. Add double crochets to the following four stitches, and two double crochets to the final stitch of the round.

- Turn the work for the third round, chain three, and repeat the previous pattern for the remainder of the round.

- Now switch colors and add five more rows using the same pattern.

- Make seven more color switches, each featuring five rounds.

Drapey, Full-Body Double Crochet Shawl

Supplies:

- Approx. 1,000 yards of size three yarn

- One 3mm hook

- Scissors and a needle

Instructions:

- Chain five and make a ring.

- For the first round, chain three and make five double crochets, and then chain two and add five double crochets to close the round.

- For the second round, work only in the back loops. Complete it by chaining three and adding a double crochet to remaining stitches until the chain space. Repeat the pattern *one double crochet, one triple crochet, chain tow, a triple crochet and a double crochet*. Finish the round by adding a double crochet to each stitch and close the final two with double crochets. This will create an increase by adding two more stitches for the next row.

- Proceed making 59 rows by repeating the previous pattern. You will create a full-body, triangular shape. Remember that the middle should always contain the same number of stitches, while the double crochets at the beginning and the ends of rows vary with the size of the row.

Lacey Fish-Net Crochet Shawl

Supplies:

- Size 3 yarn, 1,300 yards

- An H/8 hook

- A measuring tape, a pair of scissors, and a needle

Instructions:

- Chain three and close the circle with a slip stitch.

- Chain four and add a double crochet to the same stitch. Chain one and skip one stitch, add a double crochet to the same stitch. Chain one and skip the next double, add a double crochet to the bottom stitch, chain and skip one, add a double crochet, chain and skip one, add a double crochet to the next double crochet, repeat once more, and turn the work. You should have a total of fifteen stitches.

Repeat for the rest of your shawl.

chapter 10
Christmas Specialty Project

W e worked so much with clothes and household items, but those aren't the only things we can make. Here are some cute ideas for holiday projects that you can hang on your tree or your fireplace!

Crochet Snowflake Ornament

Here's how to make a simple ornamental snowflake:

Supplies:

- Size 3 cotton yarn and a 3mm hook
- One needle and a pair of scissors

Instructions:

- Make a five-chain ring.
- For the first row, chain one and add a single crochet to each ring of your chain. Finish with a slip stitch.
- For the second row, chain to and repeat five times *one double crochet into the

single crochet, six-chain, and one double into the bottom single crochet*.

- Add a double crochet to the next single, make a six-chain, and finish the round with a slip stitch.

- For the third row, chain one and repeat for five times: *a single crochet between the bottom double crochets twice, four single crochet into each chain space, a three-chain, a single crochet into the third chain from your hook, and then four single crochet into the next chain space*.

- Add a single crochet to the space between the bottom double crochets, four single crochets into the chain space, chain 20 into the chain space, and finish the round with a slip stitch.

- Fasten off your ornamental snowflake and enjoy!

Crochet Christmas Tree Ornaments

This Christmas crochet ornament will resemble a present.. Despite it looking complex as a finished product, it is simply a square made from two different colors:

Version No.1:

- Chain 13 and work six rows in double crochet.

- Create a loop to hang the ornament.

- Weave in a holiday-themed pattern that you like with a contrasting color.

Version No.2.:

- Make a magic ring and proceed crocheting in a circle until the ornament reaches the desired size.

- Create a hanging loop with the strand of yarn.

- Weave in a snowflake or another holiday-themed pattern.

Crochet Christmas Stocking

For this rustic-looking christmas stocking, you'll need the following:

Supplies:

- A total of 150 yards of size five yarn in two colors

- A 6mm hook and a tapestry needle

Instructions:

Cuff in color A

- For the first row, chain 13 and work the back chain bumps. Add a half-double crochet to the third chain from the hook and the remaining stitches.

- Next two rows, chain one and turn the work, adding slip stitches to stitches of the bottom row.

- For the fifth row, chain two, turn the work, and complete the row with half-double crochets worked into the back chain loops.

- For rows six through eight, chain one and then complete the rows with a slip stitch, again in the back chain loop.

- Repeat the same pattern for the ninth row until the 36th row.

- Once you've completed your cuff, join it together on the right side. To create an edge, work the back loops with slip stitches. This way the cuff will have a circular shape.

Stocking in color B

- All the rounds for your stocking will have 28 stitches. Each round will begin with a slip stitch, and you should turn the work to maintain the same fabric texture.

- For the first round, join the color B to the cuff, and work single crochets into the back loops.

- For the second round, chain one and repeat *single crochet, half-double, skip one* for the entire round.

- For the third round, chain one and turn. Skip one stitch, and then repeat the previous pattern until the end. Repeat the same pattern for ten more rows.

Heel in Color A

- For the first row, chain one and add 14 single crochet.

- For the second, third, and fifth row, chain one and turn, single crochet into the first stitches, and then single crochet into two stitches together twice. Finish the row with a single crochet to have 12, 10, 8, and then 6 stitches.

- For the sixth row, single crochet together two stitches and finish with a single crochet. Repeat once more for the seventh row to get two stitches.

Toes in Color A

- Repeat the same pattern for the toe section.

73

74

chapter 11

Specialty Baby Project
— Amigurumi Toys —

rochet stuffed animals are perfect gifts for babies and small children. Not only are they soft and cuddly, you can choose the yarn and colors to make sure the material is safe for the baby! Always check with the parents to make sure the child isn't allergic to any dyes or materials before starting your project just in case. When you have the all clear, choose a pattern!

Amigurumi Bear

The picture above is not the exact teddy you will be making, but it is close! Rather than a dress, you will make a scarf instead. For this adorable little Teddy, you'll need the following:

Supplies

- Three different yarns. You'll need 165 yards of medium brown medium weight yarn, 15 yards of lightweight yarn for the scarf, and three yards of black yarn for

the bear's nose.

- A 4mm hook.

- Some polyfill to stuff the bear.

- Some white felt for the eyes and some colored felt for its ears and feet.

- Scissors and a needle

Instructions

Head

- Create a six-chain ring.

- Add two single crochets to each chain to make 12 stitches.

- For the third through fifth round, add one single crochet to the first stitch, two single crochet to the next stitch, and repeat *single crochet in the next stitch, two single crochets in the next* until you finish the round.

- For the fourth round, *one single crochet in two next stitches and then two single crochets into the next stitch*.

- For the fifth round, add a single crochet to the first three stitches and then two single crochets to the next stitch. Repeat *one single crochet in the next three stitches, two single crochets in the next stitch* until you finish your round.

- For the sixth round, work single crochets into the first four stitches and then two single crochet into the next stitch. Repeat *one single crochet into the following four stitches and then two in the next stitch* until the end of the round.

- For rows seven through ten, work a single crochet into each stitch.

- For round 11, single crochet the first five stitches and add two single crochets to the next stitch. Repeat *one single crochet into the next five chains, and two into the next one* to the end.

- For round 12, single crochet into the first six stitches and add two single crochets to the next one. Repeat *single crochet to six stitches, two single crochets to the next* to the end.

- For rounds 13-19, work single crochets to bottom stitches until the end of each round.

- For rounds 20-24, begin with a single crochet into first six, five, four, three, and two stitches by rounds and repeat *single crochet into six, five, four, three, two stitches for each round* to the end. Each round should have six stitches less compared to the previous.

- Cut off the extra yarn and leave ten inches of the strand.

Belly

- Start the first round by chaining six and proceeding to work in a spiral, without joining.

- Complete the second round with single crochets into each base stitch.

- Rounds three through eight will visually expand the belly, so you'll start each round with single crochets into first two, two, three, four, five stitches by round. This will add stitches, so each of the rounds adds six more stitches to the next one. Then you'll repeat the pattern *single crochet into (by round) two, two, three, four, five stitches plus single crochet into the next stitch* until the end.

- The following 11 rounds, 8 through 19, will give the belly a flatter look, and they'll consist of single crochets into each of the 42 stitches.

- Now, it's time to narrow down the belly. You're essentially taking the same process from the top and 'mirroring,' or reversing, it for the bottom. Start the round 20, 22, 24, and 27 by adding a single crochet into first four, three, and two stitches by round, and then repeating *single crochet into next five, four, three, two* by round stitches until the end.

- The mean rounds: 21, 23, 25, 26, 28; and 28 will be done with only single crochets.

- Upon finishing row 29, fasten the work off and leave a tail.

Limbs

Great job, you've come to the easiest parts of making your bear! Now you need to make his limbs:

- Start the first round with a six-chain and proceed spiraling two single crochets for the second round so that you finish with 12 stitches.

- For the third round, single crochet into the first stitches, and then add two single crochets to the next stitch. Repeat *single crochet into the next stitch followed by two single crochets into the next stitch* to the end.

- Work four more rounds with single crochets into each stitch so that you finish with 18 stitches.

- For round nine, add a single crochet to the first stitch and then join the next two stitches with a single crochet. Repeat *single crochet in two following stitches and then joining the next two stitches with a single crochet* to the end.

- Work fourteen more rounds with single crochets into each stitch and fasten off.

- Don't forget: You need four of these pieces, and leave a strand!

Nose

You can fashion the bear's nose as you choose. Some women prefer to weave it in with black yarn, others from cut-out felt, and there's also an option to sew in a button—whatever works best for you!

Ears

- You can either make ears from other fabrics like felt, and you can also crochet ears for your bear. Here's how to make them from yarn:
- Chain six, but instead of joining the ring, proceed with spiral crochet.
- Work four more rounds with single crochets into each stitch.
- Finish the work and leave a strand so that you can join them later on. Don't forget to make two pieces!

To make the bear's tail, you can either cut out and sew in a piece of fabric or start a round of magic six-chains and proceed spiraling two single crochets into the base to create 12 stitches, and then single-crochet two more rounds to complete it. Fasten off and leave a tail.

Scarf

The final piece of crochet will be the toy's scarf. For this, make a desired-size single crochet mini scarf. My suggestion is to make a 22" scarf of desired width.

Eyes

To make the bear's eyes, you can either weave them in using a shape that you like or sew in buttons.

It's Time to Assemble Your Bear!

After you're finished crocheting all of the parts, you then need to stuff the head, body, and limbs. Sew each part shut and then sew them together. Sew the ears and the tail in place, and tie the scarf below the bear's head. Weave in any remaining strands.

Great job, you've now made your first amigurumi toy! But wait, this doesn't have to be your only toy project. You can easily turn your bear into a rabbit or a mouse by increasing or reducing the number of rows in the basic pieces. Adding length to the ears and limbs will easily turn your bear into a bunny. Reducing them, on the other hand, combined with a smaller, more extended nose, will create a mouse! If you decide to make your rabbit or mouse, don't forget to make them some whiskers and appropriate tails!

Amigurumi Bunny

Supplies:

- This adorable, chunky bunny, is made from 50g of DK yarn in the color that you choose

- You need a 2.5mmm hook

- Fiberfill

- Needle and Scissors

Instructions:

Head

- Before you start, remember that each part begins with a magic ring but without joining rounds or turning the work.

- The first round is a six-chain that spirals into the second round in which you should add two double crochets to each stitch.

- The third round features single crochets and ends with an increase— add two single crochets into the final stitch.

- The fourth round begins with an increase and features single crochets until the end while round five begins with a single crochet into the third stitch, single crochets throughout, and then ends with an increase.

- The sixth round begins with a single crochet, an increase, and then five repetitions of single crocheting four stitches followed by an increase. End the row by adding single crochets to the last three stitches.

- The seventh round repeats five single crochets with an increase for a total of six times.

- You need to add seven more rounds of plain single crochets into each of the base stitches.

- The fifteenth round repeats five single crochets followed by a decrease for six times.

- Round 16 begins with a single crochet followed by a decrease, and then five repetitions of four single crochets with a decrease. The round closes with three single crochets.

- Round 17 repeats the pattern of three single crochets with a decrease for six times, while round 18 repeats the pattern of a decrease followed by two single crochets for six times.

- The final round alternates between one single crochet and one decrease for six times.

- After completing the bunny's head, you can either weave in or attach eyes depending on the materials you chose. Remember to also make the nose and the mouth. Stuff the head and begin working on the body.

Body

- For the body, start with a six-chain spiral and then increase to 12 stitches for the second round.

- The third round repeats single crochet with an increase for six times, while the fourth round alternates increases with two single crochets for six times.

- The next four rounds are done with single crochets into each of the bottom stitches.

- The ninth round repeats twice a pattern of a decrease followed by ten single crochets while the tenth begins with three single crochet and a decrease, which you repeat four times, finishing with two single crochets.

- The eleventh row is made from single crochets while the twelfth row doubles a pattern of a decrease followed by seven single crochets. The final round requires you to repeat two single crochets with a decrease four times.

- Upon fastening off, fill the body and sew it into the head.

Limbs

- Start the second round by repeating three times: increase and a single crochet.

- Single crochet the next two rounds.

- The sixth round counts three single crochets with a decrease, followed by four single crochets.

- Add two more single crochet rows.

- For the ninth round, add three single crochets, a decrease, and a single crochet, top with two more rounds of single crochet.

- Round 12 starts with three single crochets and a decrease and ends with two single crochets. After the thirteenth round of single crochets, do three single crochets, fill the limb, and close the gap.

- Follow the same instructions for the tail as with the previous project.

Ears

For two long, straight ears, repeat the following steps:

- After the first round of six spiral chains with single crochets, add increases to each stitch in the second round followed by a single crochet three times to create a total of nine stitches. The third round requires you to do two single crochets with an increase three times while the fourth round begins with a single crochet and an increase and then repeats three single crochets with an increase twice, ending with two single crochet.

- The fifth and sixth round are done with single crochets to each stitch, and the seventh round begins with three single crochet and then a decrease and ends with 10 single crochets. The eighth round features all single crochets.

- Round nine repeats twice the pattern of a decrease followed by five single crochets.

- The next two rounds are done with single crochets while the twelfth round repeats a decrease with four single crochets twice.

- After two more rounds of single crochet, close the piece by repeating a decrease with three single crochet twice.

Amigurumi Doll

Make this adorable little doll with a 3mm hook and the rest of these supplies.

Supplies:

- Filling material
- Needle
- Yarn
- Thread or beads for eyes, nose, and

Instructions:

- Make the head, body, and limbs as explained in the previous pattern.
- Weave in strands of yarn in thickness and length that you prefer for the doll's hair.
- Weave in eyes, nose, mouth, and shoes for a livelier look.
- You can crochet a dress specifically for the doll, or you can dress her up in other small items of clothing that you have.

conclusion

Just look at your amazing work! You made a total of 30 different crochet items, samples, and swatches! In a matter of days, you went from being a complete novice to crochet to a quite successful beginner. If you've been using the patterns and taking the advice given in this book, you now probably have dozens of beautiful projects under your belt, and you're fully equipped to start learning more complex things. And you should! Crochet is all about fun, experimentation, and creative freedom to build and orchestrate stitches and chains as you see fit. The more you exercise the simple projects, the better you learn to substitute stitches, colors, and yarns, to make the work truly your own. *Crochet for Beginners* gave you the basics and taught you how to

- **Read crochet patterns.** You learned how to read diagrams, symbols, instructions, recognize repetitive sections, and, of course, select from a variety of yarns and hooks to find the material that works best for what you want to create. Now you can pick up any pattern and not only know how to make it. You can be creative with it and add changes that you want so that each of your projects are fully customized!

- **Make a ton of projects.** You learned how fast and easy it is to crochet if you plan and organize well. In truth, some of the more difficult parts about crochet include looking over diagrams and patterns and making sure you're on the right track. Hopefully, this book provided enough instructions for you to quickly grasp the structure and parts or patterns within the work so that you can break it down for yourself. That way, it becomes much faster and convenient.

- **Relax productively.** No more feeling guilty about spending your afternoon in front of the TV! With the hook in one hand and the yarn in the other, any time spent crocheting is time well spent! As the time comes to say goodbye, I want to remind you to always choose the best of the best for yourself and your loved ones. Whether it's yarn or designs, crochet gives you the freedom to make unique gifts, clothing, and family in the form of stuffed friends for your loved ones. You're not only creating art; you're making mementos that will remind everyone of how much you care about them.

Remember to be patient and kind with yourself when doing crochet! It's normal to make errors as a beginner. Relax because in crochet, nervousness only increases the chances that you'll make a mistake. Nervousness will make you clench your fists and tighten your work, resulting in too much tension and crooked work. With crochet, you can always unravel anything you don't like and start over! So be kind to yourself, take a deep breath, and relax. It's time to crochet!

references

Amberlink. (December 25, 2020). *Snowflake tree crochet winter*. Pixabay. [Image]. https://pixabay.com/photos/snowflake-tree-crochet-winter-6003786/

Anastaciaknits0. (April 4, 2015). *Crochet red black handmade textile*. Pixabay. [Image]. https://pixabay.com/photos/crochet-red-black-handmade-textile-935025/

Bilsborough, V. (April 3, 2017). *Sweater*. Unsplash. [Image]. https://unsplash.com/photos/nLNimOqmbpg

Borodinova, V. (April 23, 2018). *Woman is reading vintage book*. Pixabay. [Image]. https://pixabay.com/photos/woman-is-reading-vintage-book-3344589/

Casey, C. (2013). *All about crochet-A beginner's guide*. Lulu Press, Inc.

Congerdesign. (June 24, 2015). *Crochet blanket sofa couch ceiling*. Pixabay. [Image]. https://pixabay.com/photos/crochet-blanket-sofa-couch-ceiling-818720/

Cosh, S., & Walters, J. (2014). *The crochet workbook*. Courier Corporation.

Coudriet, J. (January 1, 2019). *Christmas Eve*. Unsplash. [Image]. https://unsplash.com/photos/zdQe7YL9Unc

Crochet puppets. Author-owned image. [Image].

Diamond stitch. (October 6, 2021). Author-owned image. [Image].

Double crochet. (October 5, 2021). Author-owned image. [Image].

Frank, J. (November 29, 2018). *Aaron at the bus station*. Unsplash. [Image]. https://unsplash.com/photos/C_H2SGZ5i-w

Free-Photos. (February 14, 2016). *Woman girl blonde shawl rings*. Pixabay. [Image]. https://pixabay.com/photos/woman-girl-blonde-shawl-rings-1149909/

Griffiths, M. (2015). *Crochet in no time: 50 scarves, wraps, jumpers and more to make on the move*. Ryland Peters & Small.

Heftiba, T. (September 30, 2016). *Women in dry foliage*. Unsplash. [Image]. https://unsplash.com/photos/w1BpjY4aH2A

Karina L. (June 2, 2020). *Crochet hook*. Unsplash. [Image]. https://unsplash.com/

photos/d1yqso_6tns

LauraMR5. (April 15, 2020). *Rabbit amigurumi snowman toy*. Pixabay. [Image]. https://pixabay.com/photos/rabbit-amigurumi-snowman-toy-5048006/

Liban, J. (March 12, 2018). *Pineapple pillow*. Unsplash. [Image]. https://unsplash.com/photos/3ugRoVpotNk

MirelaSchenk. (December 25, 2016). *Christmas decoration*. Pixabay. [Image]. https://pixabay.com/photos/christmas-decoration-1930441/

Montemari. (March 11, 2018). *Amigurumi teddy bear cuddly toy*. Pixabay. [Image]. https://pixabay.com/photos/amigurumi-teddy-bear-cuddly-toy-3250032/

Moore, M., & Prain, L. (2019). *Yarn bombing: The art of crochet and knit graffiti*. arsenal pulp press.

Olson. P. M. (October 8, 2015). *Newborn baby*. Unsplash. [Image]. https://unsplash.com/photos/EL5IhM6x9qo

Pasja1000. (January 12, 2018). *Blue wooden heart February wool*. Pixabay. [Image]. https://pixabay.com/photos/blue-wooden-heart-february-wool-3079236/

Pique stitch. (October 5, 2021). Author-owned image. [Image].

Puppets. (October 7, 2021). Author-owned image. [Image].

rocknwool. (March 3, 2020). *Cojin bamboo crochet pillow*. Unsplash. [Image]. https://unsplash.com/photos/NP1Hun_DKAA

Rosanegra_1. (June 4, 2016). *Amigurumi wrist woven child*. Pixabay. [Image]. https://pixabay.com/photos/amigurumi-wrist-woven-child-1436627/

Shappley, M. (August 15, 2021). *White and orange floral textile photo*. Unsplash. [Image]. https://unsplash.com/photos/aL2VXe-BuYE

Shell stitch. (October 6, 2021). Author-owned image. [Image].

Single stitch. (October 5, 2021). Author-owned image. [Image].

Tdfugere. (March 8, 2016). *Blanket baby ombre crochet rainbow*. Pixabay. [Image]. https://pixabay.com/photos/blanket-baby-ombre-crochet-rainbow-1245171/

Triple crochet. (October 5, 2021). Author-owned image. [Image].

Made in United States
North Haven, CT
15 December 2021